# mini EXPLORERS

# Jungle Animals

Written by: Kirsty Neale

Illustrated by: Stuart-Jackson Carter

igloo

# The Rainforest

Rainforests, or jungles, are found in many countries, including Africa, Asia and South America. They're home to a huge number of plants and animals, which all live in different layers of the forest.

The dark **forest floor** is covered with dead leaves, twigs and moss. Larger creatures, like anteaters and tigers live here.

**Many foods, including lemons, bananas,**

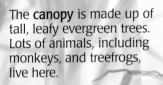

The **canopy** is made up of tall, leafy evergreen trees. Lots of animals, including monkeys, and treefrogs, live here.

Butterflies, bats and birds live in the rainforest's biggest, toughest trees. These rise above the canopy in the **emergent layer**.

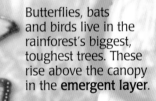

Smaller trees, ferns, shrubs and vines are found in the shady **understory**, along with many insects.

# Big Cats

Big cats are mammals. They give birth to live young, but prefer to live alone once they're fully-grown. They're meat-eating (**carnivores**) and usually hunt on their own, too.

◄ Jaguars, like ocelots, are strong swimmers and can also climb trees.

► Ocelots are one of the world's fastest wild cats. They eat mostly fish, snakes, birds and small mammals, like monkeys.

If a tiger had no fur, you would still be able

The dark circles on a **leopard's** coat are called rosettes. They provide the leopard with **camouflage**.

◀ **Tigers** are the biggest member of the cat family. Their long, strong tails are used for balance and communicating with each other.

## Camouflage

Clever camouflage helps big cats blend in with the jungle as they stalk their prey.

A **tiger's** stripes help it stay hidden in amongst the long grass.

In different parts of the world, **leopards** have darker or paler spots, depending on their surroundings. The dark circles on a **leopard's** coat are called rosettes.

**to see the pattern of stripes on its skin.**

# Frogs

The rainforest is an ideal place for **amphibians**, like frogs, to live. They breathe through their skin, which stays moist in the damp air, and feed on the forest's many insects.

**Tree frogs** have sticky discs on the ends of their fingers and toes to help them climb in the rainforest canopy.

The **poison-dart frog's** bright, beautiful markings warn predators to keep away. It's one of the most poisonous animals on Earth.

The poison-dart frog's **venom** is used on

# Lizards

Lizards are **reptiles**, with scaly skin and long tails. There are almost 5,000 different kinds, many of which can change colour so they blend in perfectly with their surroundings.

▲ Green **iguanas** live high in the rainforest canopy. They can fall up to 50ft (15m) from a tree and land safely.

**Geckos'** feet have ridges on the bottom which allow them to climb straight up trees. Some can even walk upside down!

the tips of blow-darts in South America.

# Crocodiles

Crocodiles are **reptiles**. This means they're cold-blooded and rely on heat from outside their bodies to stay warm. Most reptiles lay eggs, although their shells are more leathery than bird eggs.

Crocodiles are fearsome **predators**. They have sharp teeth and claws, and the strongest bite of any animal in the world.

Crocodiles have webbed feet, which can help them change direction very quickly when they're swimming.

**The largest crocodiles are found in India**

# Snakes

Snakes are also **reptiles**. Pythons and anacondas are **constrictors**, who grab prey in their mouth and then coil their bodies round and squeeze until it stops breathing.

The **anaconda** is an excellent swimmer. It also climbs trees where it can lie on branches and dry off.

▲ Anacondas are the world's largest snakes. Pythons are longer (up to 33ft/10m), but anacondas are wider and heavier.

A **python** can un-hinge its jaws to swallow and eat large animals, including monkeys, pigs and even antelopes.

and can be more than 23ft (7m) long.

# Monkeys

Monkeys, orang-utans, lemurs and gorillas all belong to a group of animals called **primates**. Most of them make their homes in trees in tropical parts of the world, like rainforests.

▶ **Orang-utans** sleep in large nests which they build in trees. Their name means 'man of the forest'.

## How Monkeys are like us

They use facial expressions, including angry stares and pursed lips, to communicate.

Although they often use their knuckles to help them move, monkeys can walk on two legs.

Unlike most animals, their hands have thumbs which can grip and hold things.

**A group of monkeys is called a troop, and**

▼ **Lemurs** have long, flexible tails, which they use to help them balance as they jump from tree to tree.

▶ **Spider monkeys** are named after their long, skinny arms and legs. They eat mainly fruit and nuts.

▶ **Gorillas** are the largest of the **primates**. They live on the ground, not in trees, and are plant-eating **herbivores**.

can contain as many as 500 individuals.

# On the Jungle Floor

**Capybaras** are the world's biggest **rodent**. Their closest animal relatives are rats and mice. They usually live near rivers and spend as much time in the water as they do on land.

Its eyes and ears are near the top of their head so they stay above water when the **capybara** is swimming.

**Tapirs** are a similar shape to pigs, although they belong to the same animal family as horses and rhinos.

All baby tapirs have striped or spotted coats for **camouflage**.

**Tapirs have good hearing and sense of smell**

Hungry **anteaters** sniff out termite mounds and anthills, and tear them open with their strong claws. They suck up the insects through their long nose, which works like a straw.

An **anteater's** sticky tongue is over 2ft (60cm) long and helps it collect even more ants or termites.

**Sloths** spend most of their lives hanging upside down in trees. They're well-known for being slow, and spend around 18 hours a day sleeping, which they also do upside down.

It can take **sloths** more than a month to digest food, and they only go to the toilet once a week!

**and this makes up for their poor eyesight.**

# Hiding in the Jungle

The **funnel-web** is one of the world's deadliest spiders. They like damp conditions and usually live in burrows below ground. They're named after the unusually-shaped web they spin.

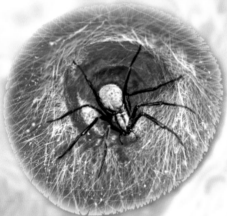

◄ Female **funnel-web spiders** spend almost their whole life inside the burrow.

**Stick insects** are sometimes called walking sticks, which is exactly what they look like. Their appearance keeps them amazingly well hidden and safe from many predators.

There are more than 3000 species of stick insect, and they range from 1″ (2.5cm) to 12″ (30cm) in length.

**Dragonflies are incredibly speedy. They**

The **praying mantis** is an impressive predator. Its large eyes and strong, spiked legs are well adapted for spotting and catching insects like moths, flies and grasshoppers.

**Praying mantis** are also cannibals. If there's no prey in sight, they will eat another praying mantis.

**Dragonflies** have four transparent wings and long, brightly-coloured bodies. Their **larvae**, which are called **nymphs**, live in water.

They feed on small insects, such as mosquitoes, ants, flies and bees.

**can fly at up to 30 miles (50km) per hour.**

# Under the Water

The **piranha** is a fish, famous for its razor-sharp, triangular teeth. It's an **omnivore**, which means it eats both meat and plants. Some piranhas also feed on fruit and seeds.

▼ They often live in large groups, not to attack other creatures, as many people believe, but to defend themselves.

They eat other fish and any wounded animals they find in the water.

**Piranhas can grow to be 18" (45cm)**

**Manatees** are also known as sea cows. They're slow-moving, peaceful and intelligent animals. They spend half their day sleeping in the water, coming up for air every 20 minutes.

▼ They live in warm, shallow water and feed on plants, including seagrasses and **algae**.

A manatee never has more than six teeth, but whenever old ones fall out, new teeth grow in their place.

long and can weigh up to 4.5lb (2kg).

# In the Canopy

The rainforest **canopy** is home to many different kinds of birds and bats.

▶ **Macaws** have two toes on each foot facing forwards and two facing back. This helps them hold their food and climb along tree branches.

There are roughly 350 species of **parrots**. They eat fruit, seeds and nuts, which they crack with their strong, curved beaks.

▶ A **toucan's** tongue measures up to 6" (15cm) long, and its beautiful bill is often half the length of its body.

**Bats are nocturnal and have webs**

▼ **Fruit bats** are also known as megabats or flying foxes. They feed on fruit and the **nectar** from flowers.

## Plants in the Canopy

The canopy is made up of many trees, including mahogany, teak, water-chestnut, balsa, cacao and rubber trees.

Air plants, related to pineapples, grow on the branches of trees.

Thick vines, like lianas, climb the canopy trees in search of sunlight.

◄ **Vampire bats** approach sleeping animals and bite a hole in their skin. Then they lick the blood which comes out.

▶ **Egrets** have long legs, sharp bills and S-shaped necks. They nest in trees near rivers or streams.

**between their fingers to help them fly.**

# Glossary

**Algae**
Small plants that live in, or near, water.

**Amphibian**
A creature that lays eggs in water, but lives on both land and water.

**Camouflage**
The way an animal's appearance helps it blend in to its surroundings in order to avoid predators.

**Carnivore**
An animal that eats meat.

**Herbivore**
A plant-eating animal.

**Mammal**
A creature that gives birth to babies, not eggs, and feeds them on milk.

**Nocturnal**
Active at night-time.

**Nymph**
The larva of a dragonfly.

**Omnivore**
An animal that eats both meat and plants.

**Predator**
A creature that hunts, kills and eats other animals.

**Primate**
A group of mammals, which includes monkeys, apes and humans.

**Reptile**
An animal that lays eggs and uses heat from outside its body to keep warm.

**Rodent**
A group of small mammals with large front teeth, such as mice and rats.

**Venom**
Poison.